Harrods
KNIGHTSBRIDGE

THE HOUSE
THAT EVERY WOMAN KNOWS

STUDIO EDITIONS
LONDON

HARRODS OBJECT HAS EVER BEEN TO SUPPLY CUSTOMERS
WITH THE BEST AT LOWEST REMUNERATIVE PRICES
HARRODS SERVE THE WORLD.
HARRODS DIAMOND JUBILEE.
COMMEMORATION YEAR.
1849 60 YEARS 1909.
CONTINUOUS PROGRESS.
1849
1909
Mr Harrod's original Premises on the Present Site in 1849.
The Stores rapidly grew and further premises were occupied.
HARRODS STORES
Harrods as it is to-day
A disastrous fire occurred in 1883, and the premises were destroyed.
As rebuilt after fire — showing the Store immediately preceeding its present magnificence.
HARRODS TEMPORARY PREMISES
After the Fire Business was carried on in Temporary Premises opposite
FROM SERVING A TINY COMMUNITY IN BROMPTON
OVER 80 DEPTS.
HARRODS NOW SERVE EVERY PART OF THE WORLD

An English Institution which commands the admiration of the world.

As far back as 1849 Henry Charles Harrod took an unpretentious grocer's shop in Brompton, and modestly founded what was destined to become the most fashionable and complete shopping centre that wit of man and power of capital in this wonderful 20th Century could devise.

To commemorate Harrods' Diamond Jubilee the Directors have issued this Souvenir, believing that customers, shareholders and friends will be pleased to possess it. It may be accepted with patriotic satisfaction, as representing the premier Store of the world, founded, built and conducted by British enterprise and capital.

RICHARD BURBIDGE, Managing Director.

HARRODS' STORES L$^{TD.}$

BROMPTON ROAD, LONDON, S.W.

Telegraphic Address: "EVERYTHING, LONDON."
Telephone No.: 3300 KENSINGTON (60 Lines).
(Private Exchange to Order Office, which Customers are recommended to ask for when ordering.

SHARE CAPITAL - - £861,400

DIVIDED INTO

360,000	Ordinary	Shares of	£1	each.
100,000	Preference	,,	£5	,,
1,400	Founders'	,,	£1	,,

DEBENTURES—

£96,550 5 per cent. First Mortgage Debentures

Interest Coupons payable on 1st April and 1st October.

RESERVE - - - - - - exceeds £680,000.

DIRECTORS.

Sir ALFRED J. NEWTON, Bart., *Chairman.*
Sir JAMES BAILEY.
Mr. HERBERT BENNETT.
Mr. EDGAR COHEN.
Mr. F. H. HARVEY-SAMUEL.
Mr. WILLIAM MENDEL.

Mr. RICHARD BURBIDGE, *Managing Director.*

GENERAL MANAGER.—Mr. R. WOODMAN BURBIDGE.

CHIEF ACCOUNTANT.—Mr. A. J. NAUGHTON.

SECRETARY.—Mr. GEORGE SHEALD.

SOLICITORS.—Messrs. McKENNA & CO., 31 to 34, Basinghall Street, E.C.

BANKERS.—Messrs. BARCLAY & CO., Ltd., 171, Brompton Road, S.W.

MAIN PREMISES—BROMPTON ROAD (87 to 135).
HANS CRESCENT (1 to 14 and 34 to 44).
HANS ROAD (1 to 23).
BASIL STREET.

WORKSHOPS— PAVILION ROAD.
DRAYCOAT AVENUE, CHELSEA.
CHAPEL PLACE.
HANS CRESCENT (34 to 42).

DEPOSITORIES—BARNES.

LIVERY STABLES—WHITE HORSE YARD, BROMPTON ROAD.
BELGRAVE YARD, EATON SQUARE.

STABLES— CHARLOTTE STREET.
PENTAGON PLACE.
LANCELOT PLACE.
BARNES.

FARMS AND GARDENS—LITTLETON and BARNES.

The Growth of Harrods' as shown by the Profits.

A GLANCE at the following statement of Trading Profits earned since the formation of the Company in 1889 will enable the reader to realise the remarkable growth that has taken place in these few years :—

For the period ending 31st December, 1890 (13 months) **£13,519**

or at the rate per annum of **£12,479**

31st December, 1891	... ...	**16,071**
31st December, 1892	... ...	**21,161**
31st December, 1893	... ...	**27,047**
31st December, 1894	... ...	**33,042**
31st December, 1895	... ...	**51,076**
31st December, 1896	... ...	**61,959**
31st December, 1897	... ...	**69,952**
31st December, 1898	... ...	**66,058**
31st January, 1900 (13 months) **£91,247**,	or at the rate per annum of	**84,228**
31st January, 1901	... ...	**87,012**
31st January, 1902	... ...	**91,335**
31st January, 1903	... ...	**110,650**
31st January, 1904	... ...	**121,180**
31st January, 1905	... ...	**135,266**
31st January, 1906	... ...	**147,401**
31st January, 1907	... ...	**162,517**
31st January, 1908	... ...	**172,837**
31st January, 1909	... ...	**198,322**

A Few Notable Events in the History of Harrods'.

1849. A small shop in Brompton is occupied by Henry Charles Harrod (the founder).

1853. Charles Digby Harrod, son of the above, leaves school and enters a wholesale grocery firm in the City.

1861. Charles Digby Harrod takes over his father's retail business at 105, Brompton Road, as "Tea Dealer and Grocer."

1866. About this time the possibilities of a department store trade presented themselves to Mr. Harrod. The West End shops were charging exorbitant prices for their goods, mainly because they were forced by customers to give from two to three years' credit, and by servants, to expend considerable sums in commissions or bribes to obtain and retain the patronage, which their masters left pretty much in their hands to bestow. Mr. Harrod seized the opportunity to give his shop and methods of business wide publicity by advertising in the *Times*, *Pall Mall Gazette*, and other papers stating that he was prepared to give better value for cash than could be obtained in any other shop in London. This move was eminently successful.

1868. William Kibble, the Grocery Buyer of the establishment of to-day, was entrusted by Mr. Harrod with the development of other departments, and started sections for Patent Medicines, Perfumery, and Stationery. This was the first practical move of Harrods' in the direction of a departmental store.

1873. The business having grown year by year, the premises were re-built on a larger scale with show rooms on the first and second floors.

1877. Mr. Harrod finds it necessary to further extend his premises, and takes over the adjoining shops, 101 and 103, Brompton Road, re-building the entire propery and adding departments for Provisions, Fruit, Flowers and Vegetables, Confectionery, China and Glass.

1883. The business at this juncture was developing so rapidly that further accommodation again became necessary, and he secured a piece of land at the back of the premises, upon which he immediately proceeded to erect an additional building; but whilst this was still in the hands of the builders (although nearly completed) a disastrous fire occurred which completely gutted the premises. On the morning following the fire Mr. Harrod took temporary offices at 78, Brompton Road (opposite the Stores), and temporary shop space at 88, Brompton Road. These were immediately re-stocked, and after strenuous and unceasing labour were actually open for business on the Monday morning following. The next day Mr. Harrod took over Humphreys' Hall, Knightsbridge, a large iron structure, and by dint of exertion and the enthusiasm which he appears to have enkindled in his staff, had it completely stocked and transformed into a shop by the following Monday. A new building was immediately started on the site of the old one, and business increased so rapidly that by September, 1884, Mr. Harrod had not only regained all the business he was enjoying previous to the fire, but had increased his turnover by more than twofold.

1884. The new premises in Brompton Road re-opened with large extensions to existing premises—the addition of Poultry, Wines and Spirits, Tobaccos and Butchers' Departments on the ground floor; Ironmongery, China and Glass, Turnery, Cutlery, Lamps, Jewellery, Stationery, and Trunks on the first floor.

1886. A further extension takes place, another 80 feet being added to the ground floor, and Departments for Carpets and Furniture opened on the first floor, whilst an extensive Warehouse for Storage was also constructed.

1889. The business was converted into a Limited Liability Company with a capital of £140,000.

1891. Mr. Richard Burbidge became General Manager of the Stores, and immediately proceeded to lay the foundation for still greater development, the success of which is so well known to our Shareholders and the public, that little need here be said beyond a reference to the table of annual profits since earned by the Company on page 3.

1897. Under his progressive management the freehold property on the north side was demolished and rebuilt in its present lavish style, and in

1901. The rebuilding of the remaining portion was undertaken, the policy being to reconstruct a complete block with an area of 120 ft. by 200 ft. each summer, so that the business might suffer as little inconvenience as possible from the operations. Thus each year the premises grew with mechanical regularity, until the gigantic fabric which is now so much admired by architectural students was completed.

In connection with this rebuilding a remarkable record was achieved, which has probably never before nor since been equalled.

The final and most westerly block, measuring 80 ft. by 120 ft. was actually demolished and rebuilt between April 27th and June 4th, a period of less than six weeks. At the time of writing this Souvenir Harrods are engaged on still further extending on the western side, where they are adding special large Showrooms for the purpose of further developing their great Furniture business.

A few of Harrods' Landmarks as Trade Pioneers:

H ONESTY.
A SSIDUITY.
R ELIABILITY.
R EPUTATION.
O RIGINALITY.
D ISTINCTION.
S UCCESS.

Pioneers of free delivery to Country.

Pioneers of Shopping by Telephone.

Pioneers of all-night Telephone Service.

Pioneers of Special Shopping Trains from the Country.

Pioneers of extra week's holiday for all Territorials in their employ.

Harrods equipped the C.I.V.

Harrods supplied the largest Carpet in the world (Olympia).

Harrods equipped the "Discovery" (Antarctic Expedition).

Harrods supplied the first Xmas Hampers for Cripples (over 3,000).

Harrods have been honoured by visits from H.M. The Queen and Royal Family, as well as by almost every Royal Personage in Europe, and many Indian and Eastern Potentates.

The Staff.

THE happiness, health and general welfare of their Staff (who number between four and five thousand) is a subject of keen and practical interest with the Directors, a typical example of their magnanimity being the granting to each member from the humblest upwards an extra week's salary, in order to celebrate the Diamond Jubilee of Harrods, Ltd.

As regards health, recognising the importance of an attractive and suitable sports ground, they some years ago acquired a large house and estate of 14 acres at Barnes, known as Mill Lodge, as a headquarters for the Harrodian Branch of the Amateur Athletic Association.

This property was formerly a residential estate. The house, now converted into club rooms, billiard room, reading rooms, etc., stands in picturesque grounds, which in their turn serve an ideal purpose as playing fields, tea gardens, croquet and tennis lawns. The company have endowed, foı the benefit of their staff, two beds at King's College Hospital, two at Guy's, and one at Seaford.

THE TERRITORIALS. The Directors have for years done everything in their power to encourage the staff to accept the duties of the citizen-soldier.

For this purpose, since 1905 they have allowed an extra week's holiday in addition to that given for the annual training, as well as special leave on all necessary occasions.

STAFF FIRE BRIGADE. A Volunteer Fire Brigade recruited from members of the staff, is a valuable Auxiliary to the permanent disposition made by Harrods, Ltd., to guard against this danger.

PENSIONS. All old employees who have devoted the best part of their lives to the service of the Stoıes and who become unfit to further prosecute their duties are pensioned off on a special pension scheme which has been successfully inaugurated.

There is a strong and well supported Prbvident Society in connection with the house, which is regularly assisted from the funds of Harrods, Ltd., who also supply a fully qualified doctor at the Stores. By joining this Society at a small weekly fee the member is safeguarded against financial worry should sickness or accident be unfortunately encountered.

THE outstanding feature of Harrods to the student of Store organization is the uniformity which has marked the development of each of the 80 various Departments gathered under its roof. It is at once evident to the casual visitor that Harrods' customers do not confine their patronage to certain sections of the Store only, but use its vast organization to supply every personal and domestic want. Thus we see the finest Grocery Shop in the world, contemporary with an equally fine Drug Shop, Tobacconist, Wine Merchants, Jewellers, House Furnishers, Stationers, Hairdressers, Drapers, etc. This uniform development is the keynote of Harrods' greatness. The firm's motto (as depicted by its trade mark) has been faithfully adhered to for 60 years. "Omnia Omnibus Ubique"—"Everything for Everybody Everywhere." Everything of the best quality, in a variety to suit all tastes and purses, and supplied to all parts of the globe.

To view Harrods for the first time is to be fascinated by its noble proportions and artistic symmetry. It is quite unique in structure, being built of rich Terra Cotta with bases of granite and fittings of Gun-metal and Mahogany. It forms one magnificent unbroken block, in shape almost a square, uniform in elevation, and comprising a series of beautiful shops on two floors, with basement for industrial purposes and storage, and upper floors of luxurious residential flats. The frontage in Brompton Road is 435 feet, Hans Crescent 365 feet, Basil Street 300 feet, Hans Road 370 feet. The shopping area is approximately 36 acres. Access is gained by handsome entrances placed at convenient distances, with uniformed attendants and pages posted at each, to control traffic and assist customers. These attendants are drawn from the Army, strong, well disciplined, attentive and courteous. Dogs of every breed may be seen chained at the entrances at all hours of the day, awaiting the return of their owners from within. The windows are lofty and deep, and form a great attraction, being regularly dressed by experts.

Inside the Emporium, one is immersed in an atmosphere of luxury and pleasure. Spacious aisles, richly carpeted, provide an ideal promenade of fashion. The air is fresh and perfectly tempered to outside conditions by a scientific system of ventilation and heating. Communication with the upper floor is established by elegant stairways and lifts, and by an electric staircase which is particularly attractive to juvenile visitors. Natural light floods every room, doing full justice to the variegated colours of the rich stocks. In the sumptuous salons one misses with relief the petty importuning to purchase which renders ordinary shopping so unpalatable. " No one ever bothers you at Harrods," is a familiar remark applied to the Store; but when service is desired, be sure it is there, courteous, quick and expert.

The interior fittings are rich and elegant, and are mainly composed of natural Ancona Walnut, Mahogany, inlaid Satinwood and Oak, rendering a light and pleasing effect. The ceilings and frescoes are worthy of special note, being painted and modelled by French Artists in the Renaissance style.

Harrods is so complete and sumptuous that one is amazed. Something more than a shopping centre, it is a recognised social rendezvous; in fact, one of the few smart rendezvous acknowledged and patronized by Society.

Regarding it in this light, a brilliant author and critic writes :—

> "*Perhaps some modern Mr. Pepys (who knows) may be chronicling Society's saunters through Harrods, the elegance of its fashions, its artistic appointments, its atmosphere of luxury and exclusiveness, for the edification of our descendants in the next century.*"

Nothing has been omitted which in the smallest way conduces to the comfort and enjoyment of patrons. Elegant and restful waiting and retiring rooms for both sexes, writing rooms with dainty stationery, club rooms, fitting rooms, smoking rooms, etc., are at one's service free of charge or question. Public Telephones are provided in all departments, a Post Office, Theatre Ticket Office,

Railway and Steamer Ticket and Tourist Office, Appointment Boards where one can leave notes for friends, a Circulating Library and Music Room, everything that modern refinement can conceive.

Mr. Geo. Edwardes was so impressed with Harrods that he made it the home of his first act in the successful Gaiety production "Our Miss Gibbs," reproducing portions of the Store with painstaking exactitude. He also entrusted Messrs. Harrods with the designing and execution of most of the dresses.

No less complete than their premises are Harrods' facilities for meeting the wants of the community. They can accommodate one with the most unexpected assistance. For example, it is possible here, with minimum trouble and expense, to insure life, property and servants, buy, sell or let houses and estates, buy or sell stocks and shares, rent a safe in which to keep valuables, open a banking account, book theatre seats, secure tickets for railway journeys, book sea passages, despatch household and other property to any part of the world. You can get your hair dressed, hire a carriage or motor car, lunch or dine on the premises, enjoy the club and reading room, join an up-to-date library, advertise in any paper, warehouse your furniture and effects, and store furs, tapestries, etc., in a specially constructed cold-air chamber.

There being more than eighty huge departments, self-contained under one roof, as well as such important outposts as the Depository at Barnes; the Livery Stables (also in Brompton Road); the Nursery Gardens and Farms at Littleton and Shepperton; the Hire and Catering Warehouse and Factories; the Motor Garage, etc., it is obviously impossible to do more than touch the fringe of them in our space.

Before taking the short pictorial tour of the popular Salons

depicted in these pages, a moment's diversion to others less known will illustrate the astonishing variety comprised in the Store.

Quite an atmosphere of romance surrounds the object of our first incursion. For a little time we desert the wealth and splendour of the ground floor surroundings, to find undreamt-of treasures beneath our feet. These are safely guarded in the temples of security known as Harrods' Safe Deposit, which rivals the Bank of England itself for solidity and strength. The marvels of its mechanism are readily explained to visitors. The Safe Deposit has been in existence for more than twelve years, and it is noteworthy that during the whole of this period, whilst valuables to the extent of many millions sterling have been deposited, nothing has been damaged, mislaid or lost in transit or otherwise. The main doors guarding the Safes and Strong Rooms have upon them, in addition to three perfectly unpickable and gunpowder proof locks, time or clock locks, so that when the Deposit is closed at night, under no circumstances can the doors be again opened until business hours next morning, not even by those in possession of the keys. The Deposit is, in a word, absolutely impregnable to thieves, fire and damp.

The Model Bakery calls for attention. It is fitted with latest machinery and equipment, and is a pattern of hygienic construction. Customers may inspect it at any time during the business hours. Here Harrods make their delicious Cakes, Bread, Pastries, etc., which are supplied in great quantities to an appreciative clientèle. A short distance from the Bakery one finds the spacious Wine and Spirit Cellars, where rare Wines and Spirits lie maturing year after year. Harrods enjoy an enormous Wine and Spirit business in all parts of the country.

The Laboratory and Dispensing Room in connection with the Drug Department is close by, and will be found especially useful to those who desire a correct analysis for any purpose of Water, Food, Drugs, Milk, etc., examination

Spirit Cellars

and advice being given at moderate charges. Here also is the Country Order Department, where orders received by post are dealt with by a trained shopping staff solely devoted to the interests of Country customers. The success of this section is quite a feature of Harrods, customers all over the kingdom ordering regularly and enjoying the same facilities as those who shop personally.

Harrods' method of dealing with orders is worthy of mention. Letters received by first post in the morning are opened immediately, the staff for this purpose being in attendance at 6 a.m. The orders for each Department are copied on separate forms in duplicate, one slip going directly to the Department for execution and the other to the Counting House to be charged. In order to convey the thousands of these slips expeditiously, a network of Pneumatic Tubes (worked by compressed air) has been installed throughout the premises. The original orders are carefully filed for reference if necessary. Telephone Orders are specialised, a large staff of experienced Telephone Order Clerks being in constant attendance.

Harrods' Exchange is open day and night, so that clients possessing telephones can make enquiries whenever the whim seizes them, assured always of prompt and courteous response.

Telephone Order Room

"HARRODS' Illustrated."

Under this title the firm issue annually their great General Price List, which has been aptly termed an encyclopædia of personal and household requirements. It is a massive volume, bound in cloth, and comprising upwards of 1,400 illustrated pages. Nearly 100 tons of paper are used in printing it, and copies are forwarded to clients in every part of the world. With the aid of this book it is quite easy to do one's shopping at home and supply every possible requirement. Copies are sent free to bona-fide householders.

HARRODS' ROYAL EXCHANGE.—A veritable Marble Palace, containing Bank, Cashier's Office, Enquiry Office, Order Office, Railway Ticket Office, Post and Telegraph Office, Wholesale, Export and Shipping and Insurance Departments.
The walls are of surpassing beauty, the finest statuary, Carrara and valuable marble from Spain, Belgium and Italy being used in the formation. Round the sides are ranged writing tables, with chairs and lounges for the use of customers. This furniture is of Spanish mahogany, upholstered in morocco leather. Stationery and writing materials are at the free disposal of visitors, together with Catalogues giving particulars and prices of any article that may be desired.

The Costume Department.

THE Costume Department (to which luxurious fitting-rooms are attached) forms a worthy entrance to the Drapery and Fashion sections. Harrods is widely known as the "Shrine of Fashion"; they set themselves to supply the most exclusive creations in fashionable attire at moderate prices, and to those who appreciate the exclusive they specially appeal. Their great forte lies in adapting beautiful Continental creations to English tastes and conditions. In originating gowns, they have also met with much success, a recent order from Mr. GEORGE EDWARDES for some forty or more Costumes for "OUR MISS GIBBS," the great Gaiety success, having been brilliantly criticised by dress experts.

A feature of this Department is the displaying of gowns on living models, some of the smartest figures in London being specially employed for this purpose.

Adjoining are the Ladies' Coat and Mantle Department, and the Misses' Costume Department.

First Floor.

The Millinery Department.

"LE dernier cri" finds a worthy home in this gorgeous section, where headgear wondrous and rare forms a study of never-failing interest. This section is typical of the many adjoining Fashion Salons—the Lingerie, Tea Gown, Underskirt, Blouse, Fur, and Umbrella Departments. Each is of palatial character, in styles Louis XV. and Louis XVI., with richly modelled and painted ceilings and fittings of rich carved unpolished Ancona Walnut of soft, silky and luxurious appearance. Most of these rooms have comfortable fitting-rooms attached.

In each a profusion of fashions are shown, and ladies may walk around in perfect freedom and select every article of attire that Fashion provides to add to nature's charms.

First Floor.

The Ladies' Boot and Shoe Dept.

A VERITABLE Palace of Footwear filled with dainty and elegant shapes and styles and every convenience for ladies to make selections. Stocks here are in very large variety indeed, the object being to fit every foot to perfection, thereby ensuring perfect comfort and freedom, and more lasting wear to the shoe.

Adjoining is the Boys' Clothing Department, where parents can equip their sons with entire satisfaction for School, College, or business. This Department supplies most of the leading Schools and Colleges in the country, and stocks all the colours and badges.

The Gentlemen's Footwear Department is downstairs, adjoining the Gentlemen's Outfitting, Hats and Tailoring Departments, for Harrods is a store for gentlemen as well as ladies.

First Floor.

The Lace and Ribbon Department.

THIS handsome Salon is similar to many others adjoining it, all devoted to the alluring charms of fashion. Rich examples of laces from all parts of Europe vie with Ribbons, Fancy Neckwear, Feather Stoles, etc. Beside it are the Departments devoted to Haberdashery, Trimming, Fancy Needlework, Artificial Flowers, Parisian Jewellery, Ladies' Hosiery, Gloves and Shawls, the whole forming a galaxy of beautiful colour and fabric of extreme charm.

Harrods' unique organization and buying powers invariably enables them to be the first in London to secure and display continental fashions. Thus the habitué of their salons is always posted with the latest and most correct ideas, a fact particularly appreciated by the London Fashion Journals.

Ground Floor.

The Silk and Silk Robe Department.

THIS, with its neighbour the Dress Material and Robe Department, forms a busy centre of the Store. Very wide ranges of fabrics are shown in both departments, whilst the ever-popular unmade Robes, which are so easily adapted to all figures, attract a large number of customers. Patterns are sent out by these sections to all parts of the Kingdom, so that country clients as well as town reap the benefit of their enterprise.

Attached to these are important Dressmaking sections, enabling customers to select their materials and have them made up on the premises, in perfect style at minimum cost. Mourning Orders are undertaken at shortest notice.

Ground Floor.

PYJAMA
SILKS
WEAR
3/6

The Household Linen Department.

THE Emerald Isle might well be proud of the esteem in which its products are held by a discerning public, judging by the enormous varieties on show in this handsome Department which occupies the north-east corner at Harrods. The curiously fine Linens are a distinctive feature, and there is besides a large space devoted to Down Quilts and Blankets and the most bewitching Handkerchiefs. Dyeing and Cleaning orders are received at a special counter in this Section.

The Manchester Department adjoins, where Calicoes, Flannels and Printed Materials are the staple items. Exclusive designs in popular Blouse and Dress Materials such as Zephyrs and Ginghams are a feature, and Harrods' predominance in this respect is again singularly evident.

Ground Floor.

Ladies' Hairdressing Courts.

UNQUESTIONABLY the finest in the world, these have excited a considerable quotum of press and public comment. Their construction is elaborate and original and the most expensive materials have been employed. The woodwork is rich polished satinwood elaborately carved in Egyptian style with introductions of superb Marqueterie panelling. A range of no less than thirty-three private Hairdressing, Manicure and Chiropody Courts are found side by side in this wonderful Saloon, as well as comfortable lounges, etc.

Adjoining is a handsome sales-room, where are sold Wigs, Transformations, Fringes, Combs, Manicure Sets, Hair Preparations, Pin Curls, Frames, Curling Pins, Hair Nets, etc., and round the corner is the Eastern or Oriental Department.

First Floor.

The Jewellery and Silver-plate Dept.

RESPLENDENT with rare gems and cunning specimens of the Silversmith's Art, the Jewellery Department occupies a prominent and favoured section of the Store. The system of competitive prices prevailing in all Departments has been particularly appreciated here, where high profits are severely barred and full advantages of keen and large buying given to patrons. The Section comprises Jewellery, Electro-plate, Cutlery, Watches and Clocks, Silver Goods and Optical. Repairs of every kind are executed on the premises. The regulating and winding of Clocks within a three-miles radius is undertaken by yearly contract, and in the Optical Section visitors may have their sight tested free and receive advice gratis.

Adjoining are the Piano and Picture Departments, the Turnery Department, Saddlery and Trunks, and French Confectionery, Forage and Coal.

Ground Floor.

CASH DESK
STERLING SILVER GOODS

The China and Glass Department.

A WELL arranged and beautiful Department which cannot fail to elicit admiration. The orderly placing of such immense varieties reflects the deft handling of masterly system and organisation. In this Department will be found most beautiful selections of China, including examples of such celebrated ware as Minton, Doulton, Wedgwood, Crown Derby, Brown Westhead, Coalport, Limoges, Dresden, etc.

In the Glass Showrooms superb sets and pieces of British and imported Glass are shown, ranging from the inexpensive machine-cut article to the most elaborate and valuable hand-cut specimens.

Adjoining is the Lamp Shade Department, Sports and Games, Toys, Baby Carriages, etc.

First Floor.

The Ironmongery Department.

DIVIDED into two sections—Artistic and Kitchen Ironmongery. The former will delight the lover of the beautiful in metal as adapted to our homes, and the latter will equally fascinate the practised housekeeper who regards utility, strength and economy as the essential details of a well-ordered kitchen. The stocks are remarkably varied, as may be gathered from the following selections :—

Sewing Machines, Lawn Mowers and Rollers, Perambulators, Garden Furniture, Wire Netting, Baths, Knife Cleaners, Mincing Machines, Household Utensils in Copper, Tin, Aluminium, and other metals, Bird Cages, Clothes Racks, Coal Vases, Cruets, Dish Covers, Enamel Ware, Fenders and Fireirons, Seat Fenders, Fire Guards and Screens, Gas Fittings, Refrigerators and Ice Safes of all sizes, Table Gongs, Jelly etc, Moulds, Ranges, Spirit Lamps, Stoves, Tool Cabinets, Weighing Machines, Wringing and Mangling Machines, etc.

First Floor.

Grocery and Provision Departments.

THE largest retail Grocery and Provision Store under one Roof in the World—surely a fitting development for the original Department on which the business was founded. Only the finest quality goods are stocked and sold at a minimum margin of profit.

Groceries and Provisions are supplied to customers all over the kingdom, and in addition these Departments purvey for Yachts, Clubs, Hotels and similar Institutions. Weekly Price Lists giving latest prices, Delicacies, etc., are posted regularly and afford practical assistance to the Housekeeper in selecting wants.

Connected with the Grocery Department are large warehouses, where enormous stocks of Groceries are stored, packed and despatched. Adjoining is the Bakery Department, where a multitudinous array of Cakes and Dainty Confections are shown. There is also a special section devoted to Wedding Cakes.

Ground Floor.

Meat, Fish & Poultry Departments.

IN these splendid and extensive Departments the interior decorations are most original and artistic. The roof comprises an ornamental glass dome, 30 ft. high, and the ceilings and upper parts of the walls are beautifully inlaid with pictures depicting hunting and sporting scenes. Absolute cleanliness prevails, hygiene being an element of vital regard. More ideal conditions for vending perishable commodities could not be imagined. Buyers in these Departments visit the markets every morning, and only the best and freshest food-stuffs are supplied. Daily Price Lists are displayed, showing latest prices. Adjoining is the French Cuisine Department.

Ground Floor.

TURKEYS
TO:..

Fruit and Flower Department.

GORGEOUS Plants and Flowers here vie with the fresh home and Colonial Fruits and form a most delightful spectacle, especially during the seasons. Many of these products come from Harrods' own Nurseries, and arrive direct in perfect condition every day. Hot-house Flowers will be arranged here for table decorations. Wedding, Court and Ball Bouquets specially supplied. Wreaths, Crosses, etc., of Natural Flowers or Holly may be ordered. Dress Sprays and Button-holes in large variety. Myrtles, Palms, Standard and Dwarf Rose Trees, Foliage and Flowering Plants of all descriptions, and Bulbs of every known variety.

Harrods undertake Floral Decorations for Balls, Receptions, Weddings, Concerts, etc., and also the hire of Palms and other Foliage Plants, by the week, month, or by arrangement, for home decoration.

PALMS

The Ladies' Club.

A FASHIONABLE ladies' paper has declared that "Messrs. Harrods have a way of anticipating the wants of their clients almost before they are aware of them themselves." As a matter of fact, Harrods go a step further and supply those wants. The fitting up of luxuriously-appointed club rooms—one for ladies, the other for gentlemen—is an example of this.

The former is situated on the first floor, and ladies desirous of becoming members are invited to apply to the Secretary, Harrods Limited.

The larger of the rooms comprising this club is furnished in Adams style in figured satinwood. The chairs are upholstered in green corded silk, tastefully decorated with applique embroidery. Indian carpets are laid over the oak parquet floor. Altogether it is a very sumptuous apartment with quite an air of welcome prevailing. The retiring-room is nicely fitted out, the effect in marble being admirable. The windows are of stained cathedral glass, while the walls are covered throughout with panelled Brecchi Sanguine, Pavannazi, Levantine marble and onyx panels, the whole rendering an unique effect.

The Gentlemen's Club

IS furnished in the style of the Early Georgian period, carried out in richly carved and moulded mahogany. It is situated on the ground floor, close to the Furniture Department. Membership is obtainable on application to the Secretary.

The Grand Restaurant.

ONE of the most fashionable and comfortable in London, and extremely popular with visitors. A recherché cuisine and expeditious service is combined with prices of a strictly moderate tendency, and an excellent wine list.

Hot and Cold Luncheons, Table d'Hote and à la carte, served from 12 till 3 daily.

Afternoon Tea is served to the strains of Harrods' Royal Red Orchestra, which plays in the pavilion from 3 till 5 daily. A feature is a special Afternoon Table d'Hote Tea, a very popular and fashionable ménage. Altogether an ideal resting and refreshment centre. Luxurious Reading and Retiring Rooms for ladies, and a Smoke Room and Lounge for gentlemen adjoin.

Ground Floor.

DEPARTMENTS AT HARRODS.

DEPARTMENTS AT HARRODS.

The House That Every Woman Knows was first published
by Harrods in 1909 to commemorate Harrods' Diamond Jubilee, 1849-1909

This edition published 1988 in co-operation with Harrods Limited by Studio Editions
an imprint of Bestseller Publications Ltd.
Princess House, 50 Eastcastle Street
London W1N 7AP, England

ISBN 1 85170 243 1

Printed and bound in Italy